jBIO
SHACKLETON

11-26-19

Doeden, Ma[tt]

Surviving Antarctica:
Ernest Shackleton
CHILDREN: BIOGRAPHY

ALTERNATOR
BOOKS™

SURVIVING
ANTARCTICA

ERNEST
SHACKLETON

MATT DOEDEN

Lerner Publications ◆ Minneapolis

Lerner Publications Company
A division of Lerner Publishing Group, Inc.
241 First Avenue North
Minneapolis, MN 55401 USA

For reading levels and more information, look up this title at www.lernerbooks.com.

Library of Congress Cataloging-in-Publication Data

Names: Doeden, Matt author.
Title: Surviving Antarctica : Ernest Shackleton / Matt Doeden.
Other titles: Ernest Shackleton
Description: Minneapolis, Minnesota : Lerner Publications, [2019] | Series: They
    survived (Alternator Books) | Includes bibliographical references and index. |
    Audience: Ages: 8–12. | Audience: Grades: 4 to 6.
Identifiers: LCCN 2018010732 (print) | LCCN 2018022401 (ebook) |
    ISBN 9781541525627 (eb pdf) | ISBN 9781541523494 (library binding : alk. paper)
Subjects: LCSH: Shackleton, Ernest Henry, Sir, 1874–1922—Juvenile literature. |
    Explorers—Great Britain—Biography—Juvenile literature. | Antarctica—
    Discovery and exploration—British—Juvenile literature.
Classification: LCC G875.S5 (ebook) | LCC G875.S5 D64 2019 (print) | DDC 919.89 [B]
    —dc23

LC record available at https://lccn.loc.gov/2018010732

Manufactured in the United States of America
1-44422-34681-6/26/2018

CONTENTS

INTRODUCTION
ABANDON SHIP

Endurance groaned and creaked. Twenty-eight men, led by explorer Ernest Shackleton, had spent nine months on the wooden ship. They were trapped in the middle of the thick ice of the Antarctic's Weddell Sea. As spring approached, the ice began to break up and move. The shifting blocks of ice were slowly twisting and crushing the *Endurance*.

The ice finally broke through the **hull** on October 27, 1915. Frigid seawater poured in through the cracks. Shackleton looked on as *Endurance* finally lost its battle with the ice that had trapped it. He gave the only order

he could: abandon ship. The men lowered the ship's three small lifeboats and then moved out onto the ice. Over the coming weeks, they watched as ice twisted their once-sturdy ship. Finally, on November 21, *Endurance* slipped below the surface.

Shackleton and his men were alone, with limited supplies. They were stranded on the ice 346 miles (557 km) from land. No one knew their location. There was no hope of rescue. After nine months trapped in the ice, their troubles were only beginning.

CHAPTER 1

TRAPPED

Shackleton was obsessed with Antarctica. The British explorer had tried and failed to be the first to reach the South Pole in 1907. Seven years later, in 1914, he wanted to be the first to travel across the frozen continent. He had funding. He had a ship. But he needed a crew.

Shackleton looked for men who were both easygoing and adventurous. He chose seasoned explorer Frank Wild as his second in command and sailor Frank Worsley as the ship's captain. He filled the rest of his crew with scientists, **tradesmen**, and even a photographer named Frank Hurley.

Australian Frank Hurley was *Endurance*'s official photographer.

Some of the crew poses on the deck of *Endurance*.

In December the crew of twenty-eight sailed from the South Atlantic island of South Georgia and headed for Antarctica's Vahsel Bay. The ship soon came upon **pack ice** floating on the surface of the sea. At first, Worsley was able to guide the ship through the ice. However, as the ice got thicker, *Endurance* couldn't break through. The crew waited, hoping for an opening, but instead, the ice pack surrounded the ship like cement. *Endurance* was trapped.

THE HEROIC AGE

Historians refer to the years from 1897 to 1922 as the Heroic Age of Antarctic Exploration. It was a time of international cooperation and competition to explore the frozen continent. The age began with an Antarctic **expedition** in 1897. A young explorer, Roald Amundsen, was a member of the first team to spend a winter in Antarctica.

In 1907 Shackleton led an expedition for the South Pole. He pushed to within 100 miles (160 km) of his goal before a food shortage forced him to turn around. He planned to try again, but Amundsen beat him there, leading the first team to the pole in 1911. It was the peak of the Heroic Age.

Once this achievement was reached, the age slowly fell into decline. This was due in part to the breakout of World War I (1914–1918) in Europe. Historians mark the end of the Heroic Age at 1922, with Shackleton's attempt to **circumnavigate** Antarctica.

Explorer Roald Amundsen and a crew member perform an experiment to prove that they are at the South Pole.

The ship drifted along with the ice. As the months went on, the crew realized the danger of their situation. Daylight hours decreased as the Antarctic winter began.

The ship was stocked with supplies, and the crew hunted seals and penguins, boosting food stores. In July the sunlight returned, but blizzards battered the ship. Despite these conditions, **morale** remained strong. The men went about their daily work to clear the crushing ice away from the ship, affectionately referring to Shackleton as Boss.

The crew found ways to entertain themselves during the holdup. They even played soccer on the ice!

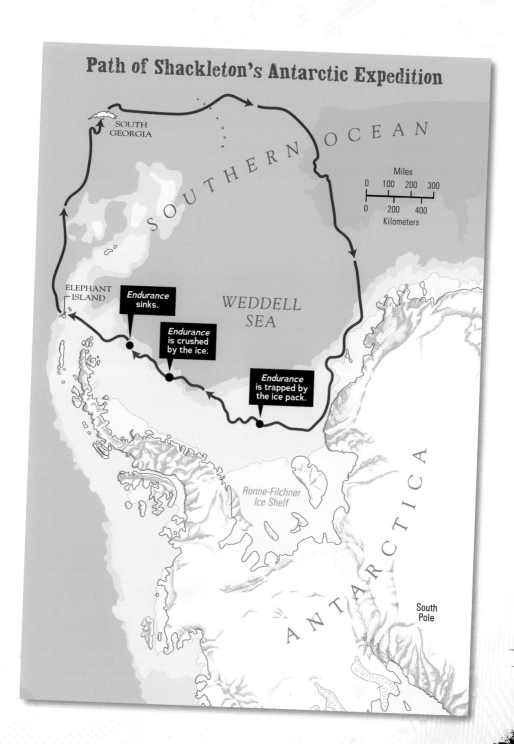

Path of Shackleton's Antarctic Expedition

SOUTH GEORGIA

SOUTHERN OCEAN

Miles
0   100   200   300

0   200   400
Kilometers

ELEPHANT ISLAND

Endurance sinks.

Endurance is crushed by the ice.

WEDDELL SEA

Endurance is trapped by the ice pack.

Ronne-Filchner Ice Shelf

ANTARCTICA

South Pole

In September, Antarctic spring arrived. The melting ice fractured and shifted. Massive **ice floes** slammed and ground into one another, putting pressure on the ship's hull. "The noise resembles the roar of heavy, distant surf," Shackleton wrote. "Standing on the stirring ice one can imagine it is disturbed by the breathing and tossing of a mighty giant below."

Crew members attempt to clear a path in the ice for *Endurance* but are unsuccessful.

Endurance could not withstand the crushing force of the pack ice.

In October, *Endurance* began to break apart. The men fled onto the ice, where they set up camp. The ship finally sank in November. The crew had only one choice. They would hike west, hopeful that the ice pack would drift toward the Antarctic mainland.

CHAPTER 2
FROM ICE TO SEA

In December 1915, the crew set out on their march. They tried dragging the lifeboats. After several days of marching, Shackleton realized that the effort was hopeless. He gave the order to stop and make a new camp. The crew had to wait for the ice to open.

The crew struggles to drag a lifeboat across the ice. This was the only way the lifeboats could travel until the ice broke up enough for the crew to set sail.

Food grew scarce. There wasn't enough left to feed both the men and the dogs, so the crew was forced to shoot the animals.

On April 7, 1916, small, isolated Elephant Island appeared on the horizon. Two days later, the ice broke away enough to allow the lifeboats to reach open water. The crew rowed for the island.

The men were tired and starving. Yet they rowed for seven days. They were exhausted when they reached the shores of Elephant Island on April 16. For the first time in 497 days, they set foot on solid ground.

The men celebrated. Yet their situation was still grim. Elephant Island was far from civilization. No one knew they were there, and Shackleton knew rescue would not come. If Shackleton did not act, the men would starve. He ordered **shipwright** Harry McNish to prepare the sturdiest of the three boats for another voyage.

Members of the expedition attempt to make a shelter from the ice on Elephant Island.

Seven days after arriving on Elephant Island, Shackleton and a crew of five left aboard the ship *James Caird*. Their destination was South Georgia, 800 miles (1,287 km) across some of the stormiest seas in the world. The 22-foot (7 m) lifeboat would go up against massive waves. And the crew would be guided by only the sun and stars.

Wild stayed behind, in charge of the remaining men. They turned the other two boats into a small shelter and hunted penguins and seals for food. All they could do was try to survive, with hopes that Shackleton's journey would be a success.

CHAPTER 3
THE JOURNEY

By the time Shackleton and his men left Elephant Island, their expedition had lasted for more than five hundred days. But the most dangerous part was still ahead.

Wind and waves battered the small boat. Everyone and everything was wet all the time. In the cold Antarctic air, **frostbite** was a constant danger. Thick ice formed on the hull of the boat, weighing it down. The crew had to throw much of what they had, including spare oars and sleeping bags, overboard to lighten the load. They lived on small **rations**.

Thick clouds blocked the sky. The crew could only guess their location. Finally, seven days into the journey, the sky cleared long enough for Worsley to measure the sun's position and calculate their location. Worsley estimated that they'd traveled almost half the distance to South Georgia.

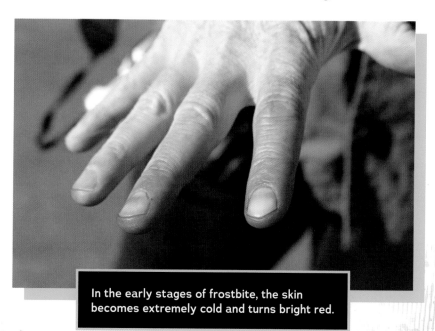

In the early stages of frostbite, the skin becomes extremely cold and turns bright red.

SURVIVAL GEAR

The crew of the *James Caird* made their journey to South Georgia with only the sky as their guide. Captain Frank Worsley used a tool called a sextant to find his way. This instrument measures the distance between objects in the sky. Using these measurements, he calculated their latitude and longitude and determined their location.

On the eleventh day, Shackleton thought he saw a break in the clouds ahead. It took him a few moments to realize he was looking at a giant wave. "During twenty-six years' experience of the ocean in all its moods I had not encountered a wave so gigantic," Shackleton wrote. "We felt our boat lifted and flung forward like a cork in breaking surf. . . . But somehow the boat lived through it."

The *James Caird* had to travel through the Southern Ocean with some of the roughest waters in the world.

To reach civilization, Shackleton and his men would need to make the perilous and grueling hike through the interior of South Georgia.

On May 8, the crew spotted land. It was South Georgia. Strong winds prevented them from making it to the island right away. They remained at sea, tossed in the churning waves, until they were finally able to reach shore two days later.

Against all odds, the tiny *James Caird* had arrived at South Georgia. However, the men had landed on the uninhabited west side of the island. They would still have to walk to reach the whaling stations on the east side.

Shackleton, Worsley, and Second Officer Tom Crean made the hike, leaving the other three behind. It took them thirty-six hours. They climbed rugged mountains, hiked over glaciers, and plummeted straight down a towering waterfall to reach their destination. On May 20, the three exhausted explorers walked into Stromness whaling station. After more than five hundred days fighting to survive, they had made it.

Leith Harbour was another whaling station in South Georgia at the time of Shackleton's expedition. Shackleton, Worsley, and Crean would have seen a similar sight as they descended from the mountains to Stromness.

CHAPTER 4

RESCUE AND RETURN

Shackleton wanted to rescue the rest of his crew as quickly as possible. A whaling ship sailed around the island to pick up the three men on the other side.

Rescuing the survivors on Elephant Island was more difficult. Shackleton tried to sail to the island three times. Pack ice blocked the way each time. Finally, in August, Shackleton made a fourth attempt. This time, he pushed through. On August 30, the men stranded on Elephant Island spotted the ship. Their boss stood on the bow.

Against all odds, Shackleton had not lost one member of *Endurance*'s crew. The men returned to Britain, where they met with further disaster. World War I raged across Europe. Men were fighting and dying in unimaginable numbers.

After more than four months, the rest of Shackleton's crew was rescued from Elephant Island.

SHACKLETON ON THE SCREEN

In 2002 Britain's Channel 4 released a two-part miniseries titled *Shackleton*. The drama told the true story of the *Endurance*'s failed expedition and the survival of its crew. The miniseries was well received by fans and critics and was nominated for seven Primetime Emmy Awards. It won in two categories: Outstanding Cinematography for a Miniseries or a Movie and Outstanding Music Composition for a Miniseries, Movie or a Special.

Kenneth Branagh (*front*) and other members of the miniseries *Shackleton* film the treacherous voyage through the Southern Ocean.

Many of *Endurance*'s crew—Shackleton included—rushed to enlist in the army. Not all of them survived the war. Seaman Timothy McCarthy died defending an oil tanker in 1917. Third Officer Alfred Cheetham died just weeks before the conflict ended.

With the war over, Shackleton once again set his sights on Antarctica. In 1921 he led a new expedition south aboard a ship named *Quest*. This time, his goal was to circumnavigate the Antarctic continent. Eight members of *Endurance*'s crew sailed with him, including Wild, Worsley, and surgeon Alexander Macklin.

Shackleton and his 1921 crew prepare to face the Antarctic aboard *Quest*.

Early on January 5, 1922, *Quest* floated off the shores of South Georgia. Feeling ill, Shackleton summoned Macklin to his cabin. Soon after, the explorer's heart failed. Shackleton died in Macklin's arms. He was forty-seven years old. His death marked the end of the Heroic Age of Antarctic Exploration.

Shackleton was buried on South Georgia. His gravestone faces south, toward Antarctica.

SURVIVING DEADLY SITUATIONS

All twenty-eight members of *Endurance* survived, despite facing the longest of odds. They took some basic actions that helped them survive.

1. No matter how bad things get, stay positive. Even as *Endurance* crumbled, Shackleton focused on what he would do next to survive.

2. Sometimes you have to make hard decisions. For many of the crew, the decision to put down the expedition's dogs was difficult. But Shackleton made a tough choice that may have saved their lives.

3. Use whatever is available. The crew stretched its supplies by hunting penguins and seals. Antarctica offered little in the way of help, but they took advantage of all they could.

4. Rely on yourself. When the crew reached Elephant Island, they could have just waited and hoped for rescue. If they had waited, though, it's unlikely any of the men would have survived.

5. Be careful with your supplies. Twenty-eight men survived more than five hundred days in the frozen Antarctic. They did it by carefully rationing what they had.

6. Do your best to stay warm. People don't last long in cold weather unless they work hard. Dress in layers. Light a fire whenever possible. And most of all, stay dry.

SOURCE NOTES

12 Ernest Shackleton, *The Heart of the Antarctic and South* (London: Wordsworth Classics, 2007), 450.

21 Shackleton, 562.

GLOSSARY

circumnavigate: to sail all the way around a landmass

expedition: a journey or trip taken for a specific purpose

frostbite: injury to body tissues, usually skin, caused by extreme or prolonged exposure to cold

hull: the main body of a ship

ice floes: large, flat, free-moving pieces of floating sea ice

morale: the feelings of confidence and enthusiasm of a group of people

pack ice: large masses of ice that float in Arctic and Antarctic waters

rations: fixed amounts of a supply, such as food or water, given to each person daily

shipwright: a crew member in charge of fixing and maintaining a ship

tradesmen: people with specific sets of skills for a certain task, such as carpentry

FURTHER INFORMATION

Bluthenthal, Todd. *The South Pole*. New York: Gareth Stevens, 2018.

"Chasing Ernest: A Journey to South Georgia to Find the Ghost of Shackleton"
https://www.popularmechanics.com/adventure/outdoors/a26938/south-georgia-island-ernest-shackleton/

Ducksters Geography: Antarctica
http://www.ducksters.com/geography/antarctic.php

Loh-Hagan, Virginia. *Ernest Shackleton: Survival in the Antarctic*. Ann Arbor, MI: Cherry Lake, 2018.

McCarthy, Tom. *Survival: Real Tales of Endurance in the Face of Disaster; True Stories*. White River Junction, VT: Nomad, 2016.

Nagelhout, Ryan. *The Race to the South Pole*. New York: Gareth Stevens, 2015.

NOVA Online: Shackleton's Voyage of Endurance
http://www.pbs.org/wgbh/nova/shackleton/

What's It like in Antarctica?
https://www.coolantarctica.com/Antarctica%20fact%20file/antarctica%20environment/whats-it-like-in-Antarctica.php

INDEX

PHOTO ACKNOWLEDGMENTS

Image credits: EITAN ABRAMOVICH/AFP/Getty Images, p. 1; Universal Images Group Editorial/Getty Images, pp. 4–5, 28; Paul Popper/Popperfoto/Getty Images, p. 5; Popperfoto/Getty Images, p. 6; Scott Polar Research Institute, University of Cambridge/Hulton Archive/Getty Images, pp. 7, 8, 10, 12, 23; Bettmann/Getty Images, p. 9; Laura Westlund/Independent Picture Service, p. 11; ullstein bild Dtl./Getty Images, pp. 13, 27; Hulton Archive/Getty Images, pp. 14, 15; Library of Congress (LC-USZ62-10324), p. 16; Library of Congress (LC-USZ62-9523), p. 17; Barcroft Media/Getty Images, p. 18; tome213/Shutterstock.com, p. 19; Scorpp/Shutterstock.com, p. 20; VW Pics/Universal Images Group Editorial/Getty Images, p. 21; Wolfgang Kaehler/LightRocket/Getty Images, p. 22; Tom Stoddart/Hulton Archive/Getty Images, pp. 24, 26; Royal Geographical Society/Getty Images, p. 25. Design elements: sl_photo/Shutterstock.com; Miloje/Shutterstock.com; Khvost/Shutterstock; Redshinestudio/Shutterstock.com; Milan M/Shutterstock.com; foxie/Shutterstock.com.

Cover: Library of Congress (LC-USZ62-17176) (ship); Bob Thomas/Popperfoto/Getty Images (Shackleton).